MAKING CRAZY FACES AND MASKS

Design   David West
               Children's Book Design
Designer   Keith Newell
Editor   Michael Flaherty
Photography Roger Vlitos

© Aladdin Books 1992

First published in
the United States in 1992 by
Gloucester Press
95 Madison Avenue
New York, NY 10016

Library of Congress Cataloging-in-Publication Data

Green, Jen.
    Making crazy faces and masks / by Jen Green.
        p.   cm. — (Why throw it away?)
    Includes index.
    Summary: Suggests projects involving creative
face painting and the making of masks and disguises,
using readily available materials.
    ISBN 0-531-17365-8
    1. Mask making—Juvenile literature. 2. Face
painting—Juvenile literature. [1. Mask making. 2.
Face painting.] I. Title. II. Series.
TT898.G75   1992
745.5—dc20   92-9813   CIP   AC

Printed in Belgium

Why throw it away?

MAKING CRAZY FACES AND MASKS

JEN GREEN

GLOUCESTER PRESS: New York: London: Toronto: Sydney

CONTENTS

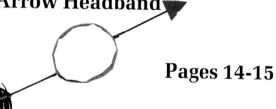

INTRODUCTION

This book will show you how to make your own collection of masks and crazy faces. With a mask you can disguise yourself and take on a whole new identity! Eleven different masks and faces are introduced in this book, and each is explained in easy stages. There are also more ideas about how you can adapt these projects, bringing in your own imagination to create new characters. Remember, in a mask you can be anyone or anything you choose!

Other ideas

All the masks shown here can be made with everyday junk that is usually thrown away. Each project includes a list of junk items used to make the model. Gather your materials together before you begin. If you don't have one of the items suggested, you may have something else that will do just as well.

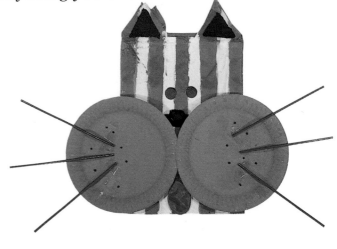

Your junk box

Start your own collection of junk now. Save any materials that might come in handy, and ask your family to pass junk on to you rather than throw it away. Make sure your materials are clean before you store them in plastic bags or cardboard boxes. For more ideas about collecting junk, see page 29.

CRAZY CLOWN

This happy clown face is built on a paper plate base. You can decorate the plate with different materials to create other faces, either human or animal.

2 Cut out and tape on a sad or smiling paper mouth. The clown's hat is a small tinfoil tray. Cut out a small paper flower for the hat, and tape it on. Tape or glue on strands of yarn for the hair.

3 Attach the hat to the clown's head with tape or a paper clip. Make a small hole on each side of the face, under the hair. Measure a piece of string or elastic to go around the back of your head. Thread it through the holes, and knot the ends.

1 This paper plate mask will fit over your face. To make eyeholes, look in a mirror and measure the distance between your eyes with a ruler. Mark your measurements on the mask and pierce the eyeholes. Cut shapes for the eyes from colored paper. Cut out the pupils. Tape on the eyes and a plastic lid for the nose.

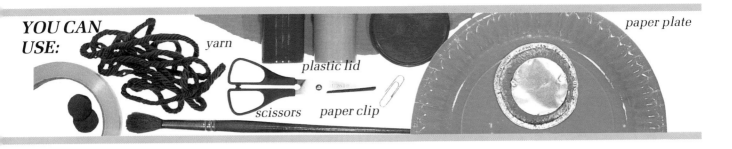

If you haven't got a paper plate, make a cardboard circle instead. Draw around a circular object on cardboard and cut out the shape with scissors.

A paper plate can form the basis of many other masks. The junk items you have collected may suggest a character to you. You could try a chef, pirate, burglar, bandit, police officer, a cowboy or cowgirl.

7

GINGER CAT

Paper bags make good masks that fit right over your head. The design shown here can easily be adapted to make many animal characters.

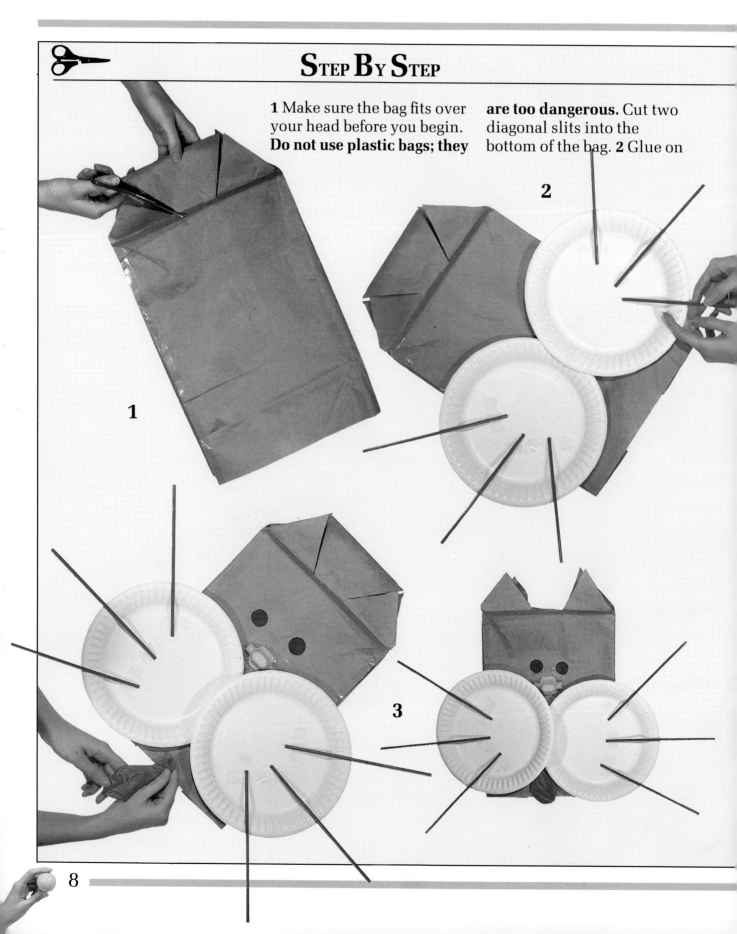

STEP BY STEP

1 Make sure the bag fits over your head before you begin. **Do not use plastic bags; they are too dangerous.** Cut two diagonal slits into the bottom of the bag. **2** Glue on

1

2

3

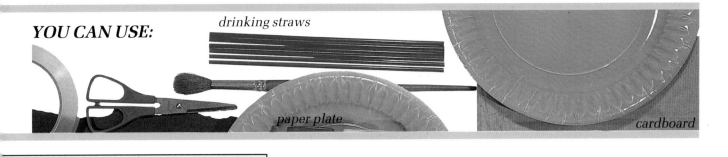

drinking straws

paper plate

cardboard

two paper plates for the cat's cheeks. You could also attach them with double-sided tape (see page 28). Tape on drinking straws for the cat's whiskers.

3 Cut a section from an egg carton to make the nose. Tape on a red balloon for the tongue. Mark eyeholes as you did for the clown mask. Cut small black paper circles for eyes, and glue them on the points you've marked. Pierce through the eyes with scissors when the glue is dry.

Decorate your bag mask with thick poster paint. You could make your cat a ginger tom, or a tabby cat with brown and black stripes.

This mask can be adapted to make a dog, a squirrel, and many other animals. You could try a tiger, or a lion with a mane of woolly strands.

You could use a cork, bottle top, or plastic cup to make the nose. You could use pipe cleaners to make whiskers, and cardboard for the nose.

ALIEN FROM OUTER SPACE

This scary alien has a single eye in the middle of its forehead, and jagged teeth.
You can adapt this design to make a robot and other space monsters.

STEP BY STEP

1

2

3

4

YOU CAN USE:

cardboard packet

plastic bottle
three toilet
paper tubes

garden sticks

egg carton

1 Cut an egg carton in half to form the alien's head. The ears are two toilet paper tubes. Cut a series of slits into one end of both tubes. Splay the cut ends flat, and tape them to the sides of the egg carton (see Practical Tips on page 28). Pierce two holes in the top of the head. Push through two sticks to make antennae. 2 Wind tape around the sticks on either side of the egg carton, to anchor the antennae in place. 3 Tape a cardboard box onto the egg carton to make the alien's jaw. For the nose, cut off the top of a plastic bottle. Cut flaps into the end and fold them over, as you did for the ears. Tape on the nose. 4 Cut another cardboard tube in half and cut out a line of jagged teeth. Tape the teeth onto the jaw. Tape on the lid of a plastic bottle to make the eye. Mark and pierce eyeholes as you have before. Make holes in the sides of the mask, and thread through string or elastic to fit around your head.

The basis of this mask can be a cardboard box of any size, an egg box or even a paper plate.

Your junk box may have other ingredients that can be used to make different alien faces. Plastic cups or even rubber gloves could be used for ears. Straws could be used for antennae. Some aliens do not have eyes, nose, and mouth arranged on the face in the same positions as we humans do.

WACKY SPECS

These zany glasses are easy to make and fun to wear. Their brightly colored eyeballs bounce crazily, and pop out on long, springy stalks.

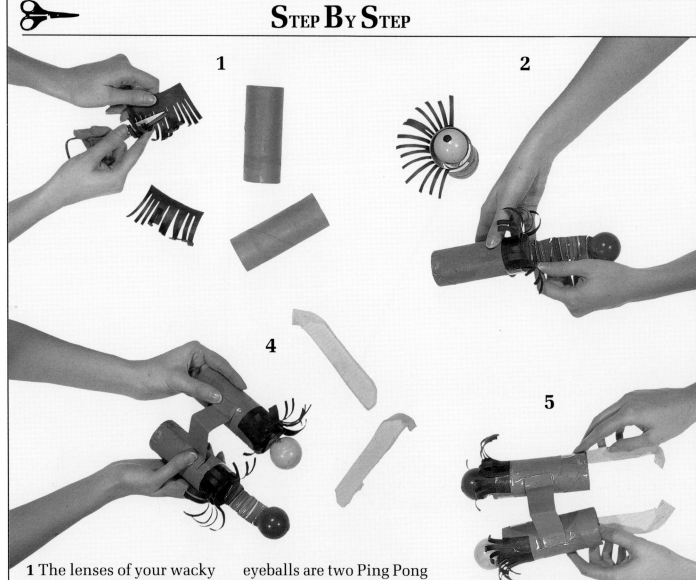

1 The lenses of your wacky specs are two toilet paper tubes. Cut two rectangles of colored paper to make eyelashes. Fringe the paper with scissors, cutting a series of slits down one side as shown. Roll the fringe around a pencil or around your scissors, to make the eyelashes curl up.
2 Tape the eyelashes around one end of both tubes. The eyeballs are two Ping Pong balls. Cut two long, narrow strips down the side of a plastic bottle to make stalks for the eyeballs. The strips should fit inside the tubes. Crease the strips into accordion folds. Tape an eyeball to one end of each.
3 Push the stalks through the tubes. Secure them inside the tubes with tape. Push the eyeballs into the tubes and make sure they pop out freely!
4 Cut a strip of thick cardboard to make the bridge between the lenses. Tape on the bridge. Cut long strips from cardboard or from the lid of an egg carton, to make earpieces, curved to fit around your ears.
5 Tape them on as shown.

YOU CAN USE:

two toilet paper tubes

Ping Pong balls

paper

3

Paint your specs with bright poster paint. To make the paint stick to plastic surfaces like the eyeballs, squirt a little dishwashing liquid into the water you use to dilute the paint.

Pierce a hole in the ends of the earpieces, and thread string or elastic through to fit around your head.

Freehand

Arrow Headband

Horrify your friends and family with this lifelike arrow headgear and its blood-soaked bandage. It can easily be made into a sword or dagger wound.

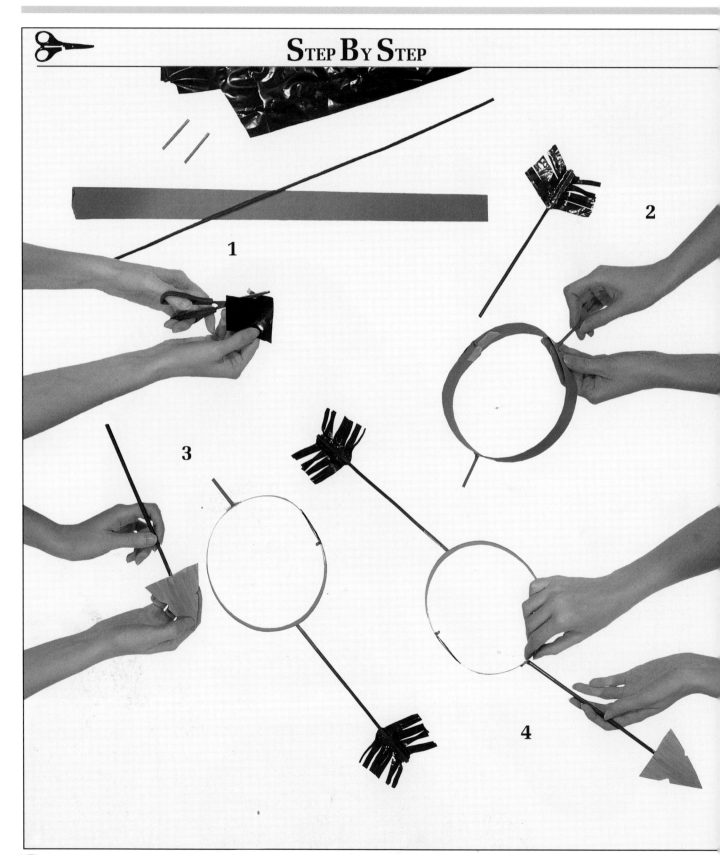

1

2

3

4

YOU CAN USE:

cardboard

drinking straws

newspaper

trash can liner

garden stick

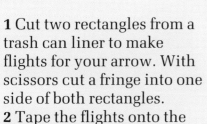

1 Cut two rectangles from a trash can liner to make flights for your arrow. With scissors cut a fringe into one side of both rectangles.
2 Tape the flights onto the end of a piece of stick. To make the bandage, fold a sheet of newspaper into a long strip. Bend it around your head and tape it together to fit you exactly. Cut two short pieces of drinking straw. Cut slits into one end of each and splay these ends flat (see page 28). Tape them on opposite sides of the bandage. The flighted end of the arrow fits into one straw. To make the point of

the arrow, cut out two triangles of cardboard. Glue them together on either side of another piece of stick.
3 Cut small nicks into the arrowhead to make it look really authentic. **4** Slot the stick into the other straw.

Paint the bandage white with fine black lines so it looks as if it has been wound around your head. Paint red blood dripping from the wounds where the arrow has pierced through your head!

You may want to moan and groan while you are wearing this headgear, to make it even more convincing!

15

STEAMSHIP HAT

This wonderful hat will create a stir at parties and get-togethers. It is light and made to fit your head exactly.

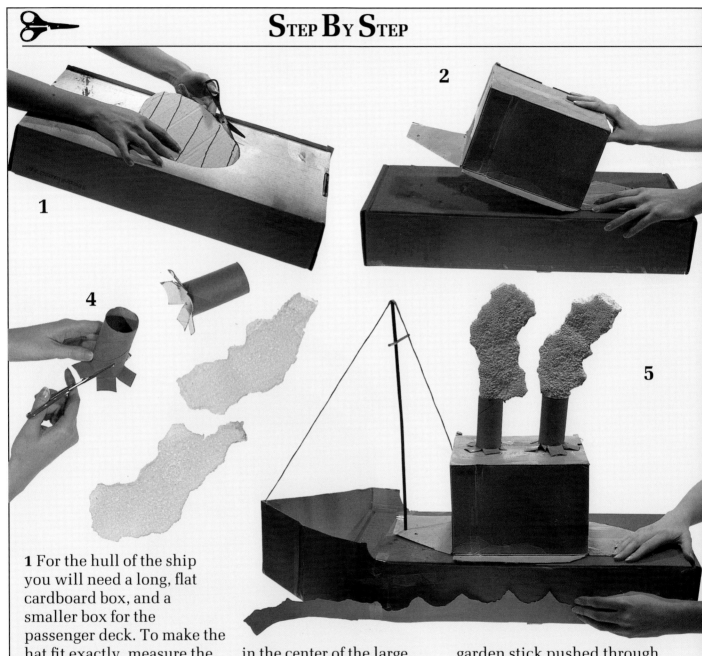

1 For the hull of the ship you will need a long, flat cardboard box, and a smaller box for the passenger deck. To make the hat fit exactly, measure the dimensions of your head, or get someone to draw around it on a piece of paper. Mark your measurements on the bottom of the flat box. Then cut out a hole for your head. Turn the box over. **2** Open the smaller box and place it in the center of the large one. Trim the flaps of the small box and tape them to the large one. **3** Cut a long cardboard strip to make the prow (front) of the boat. Fold the strip in half and tape the ends to the hull. The mast of the ship is a garden stick pushed through a small hole in the top of the flat box. Cut a straw in half to make a crosspiece for the mast. Pierce a small hole through the straw so that you can thread it onto the mast. Measure and cut a length of string for the

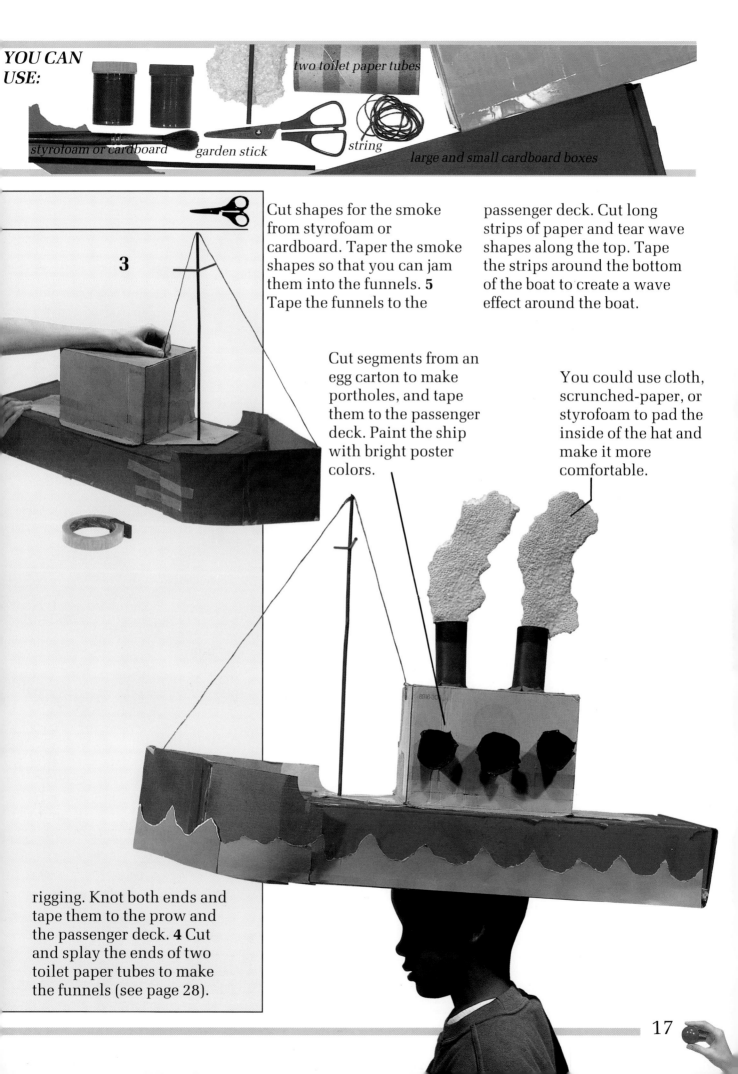

styrofoam or cardboard   *garden stick*   *string*   *two toilet paper tubes*   *large and small cardboard boxes*

3

Cut shapes for the smoke from styrofoam or cardboard. Taper the smoke shapes so that you can jam them into the funnels. **5** Tape the funnels to the passenger deck. Cut long strips of paper and tear wave shapes along the top. Tape the strips around the bottom of the boat to create a wave effect around the boat.

Cut segments from an egg carton to make portholes, and tape them to the passenger deck. Paint the ship with bright poster colors.

You could use cloth, scrunched-paper, or styrofoam to pad the inside of the hat and make it more comfortable.

rigging. Knot both ends and tape them to the prow and the passenger deck. **4** Cut and splay the ends of two toilet paper tubes to make the funnels (see page 28).

17

ANIMAL PARTY MASKS

Half-masks were traditionally worn at masquerades or masked balls. These animal faces are made using the half-mask pattern on page 31.

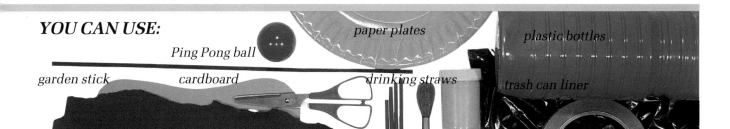

YOU CAN USE:

Ping Pong ball

paper plates

plastic bottles

garden stick   cardboard   drinking straws   trash can liner

To make the mouse:
1 Trace the mask on page 31 onto cardboard, and cut it out. Cut off the neck of a plastic bottle for the nose. Cut a slit in the back of it. **2** Slot the mask into the slit. Cut and splay the ends of six straws, and tape them to the nose for whiskers. Cut and tape on paper teeth. Add a Ping Pong ball nose. **3** Tape a cane to the nose, to hold the mask to your face.

To make the elephant:
1 Tape two paper plates to the mask for the elephant's ears. Cut off any cardboard that may cover the mask's eyeholes. **2** Cut off the top of a small plastic bottle for the trunk. Cut slits into the sides, and slot the trunk onto the mask. Tape on a stick.

To make the crow:
1 Cut out the feathers from a plastic trash can liner, using the pattern on page 31. Tape straws to the back of the feathers. **2** Cut a long triangle of cardboard for the beak, and cut nostrils. Fold the beak in half. Cut a short slit into it and fold the ends over. **3** Tape the ends to the mask. Tape on a stick.

Your junk box may contain bits and pieces that suggest other animals for you to try.

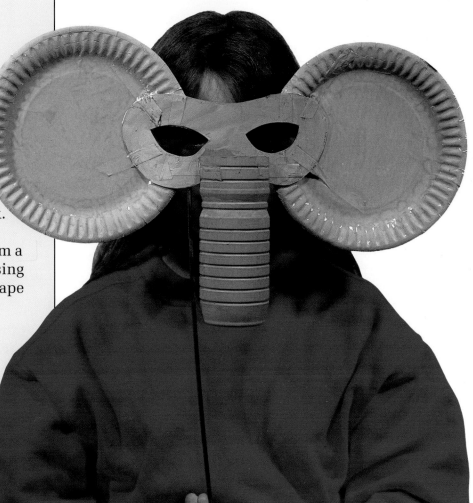

ASTRONAUT'S HELMET

This mask, a must for all space games, is based on a shell made of papier mâché. It is a vital piece of equipment when visiting alien worlds.

You could cut zigzag shapes from paper and glue them on to decorate the visor.

You could add a stars and stripes flag, painted on or made with pieces of straw.

Measure and pierce two small eyeholes in the mask with scissors. Alternatively, you could make the visor from transparent plastic so that you can see out more easily.

1 To make papier mâché, mix flour and a little water in a bowl, until you have a thick paste. Tear a newspaper into strips. Blow up a balloon and stand it in another bowl. Dip a strip in the paste, run it through your fingers to remove excess paste, and lay it on the balloon. Repeat this until the top half of the balloon is covered with at least three layers of newspaper. Leave it to dry overnight. Burst the balloon. **2** Trim the bottom of the papier mâché shape flat with scissors. Draw on the shape of the visor, and cut it out with scissors. **3** Cut two segments from an egg carton to make earpieces, and tape them on the sides of the helmet. **4** Cut out a circular piece of trash can liner to make the visor, and tape it inside the helmet. **5** The astronauts's eyes are two Ping Pong balls, and the nose is a cork. Cut eyebrows from an egg carton and tape all these features to the visor. Splay one end of a drinking straw, and tape it to the top of the helmet to make a radio receiver. Pierce a hole through the straw, cut another straw in half and push it through the hole, to form a crosspiece.

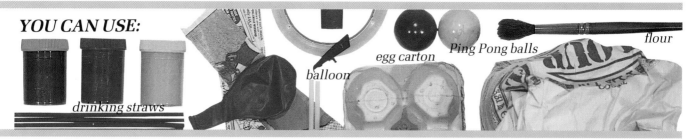

drinking straws

balloon

egg carton

Ping Pong balls

flour

STEP BY STEP

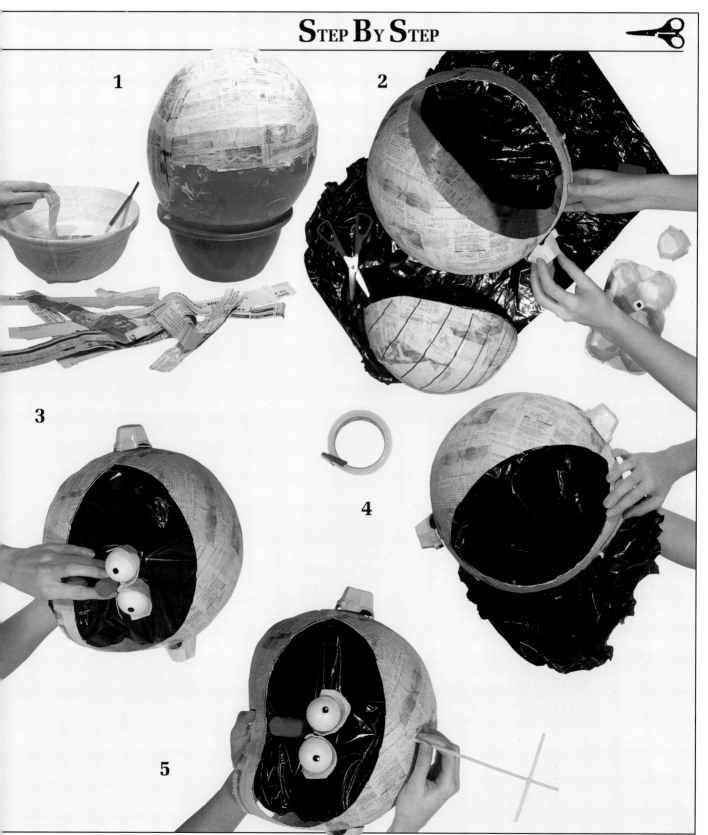

1

2

3

4

5

VIKING HELMET

The Vikings were a warlike people from Scandinavia who pillaged and plundered the coasts of Europe in their longboats in the 9th and 10th centuries.

You could make the hair and moustache from strands of yarn or even string.

Segments cut from a chocolate box tray could be used to decorate the helmet.

1 To make the papier mâché shell see pages 20-1. Blow up a balloon and stand it nozzle upward in a bowl. Dip the paper strips into the paste, and lay them on the balloon. Continue until the end of the balloon is covered with at least three layers of newspaper. 2 Leave it to dry overnight, then pop the balloon. Trim the rim with scissors. Make two horns for the helmet from paper cones (see page 28). Cut slits into the bottom of the cones, to create a series of flaps. 3 Tape the horns by the flaps onto the papier mâché shell. Cut a rectangle of cardboard to make your noseguard. Cut a strip of colored paper to make the hair. Fringe the paper with scissors. 4 Tape the fringe inside the helmet. 5 Cut a smaller strip of paper to make a moustache. Fringe both sides of the strip towards the middle. Roll it up and tape it to the bottom of the noseguard. Tape the noseguard inside the front of the helmet. Cut segments from an egg carton to decorate the front of the helmet, and tape them on.

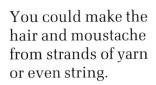

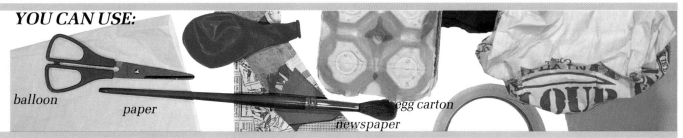

balloon

paper

newspaper

egg carton

STEP BY STEP

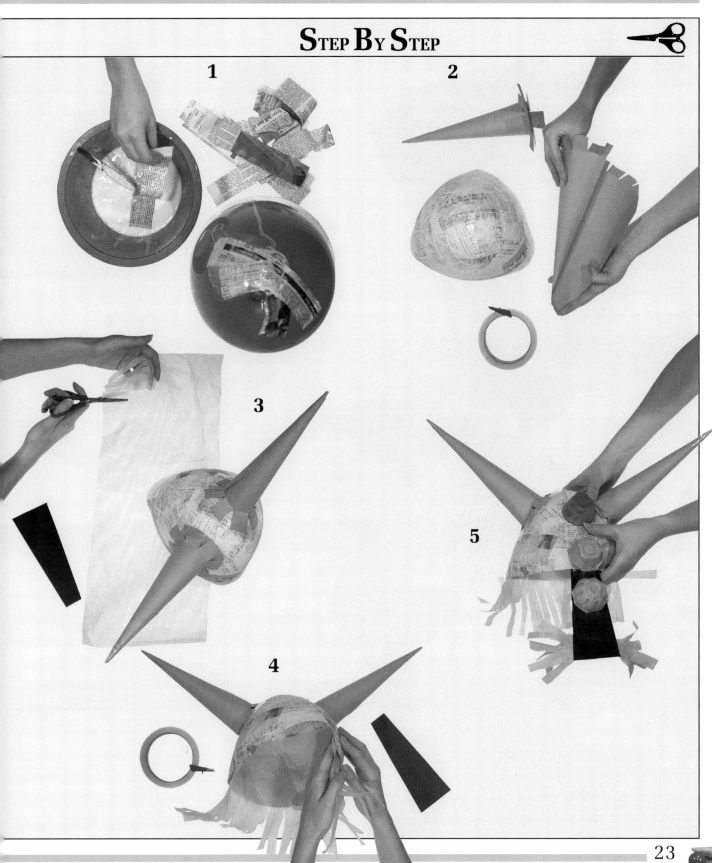

1

2

3

4

5

JESTER'S HAT

In medieval times, jesters were professional clowns hired to entertain lords and ladies at court. You will need a good supply of jokes when you wear this mask!

STEP BY STEP

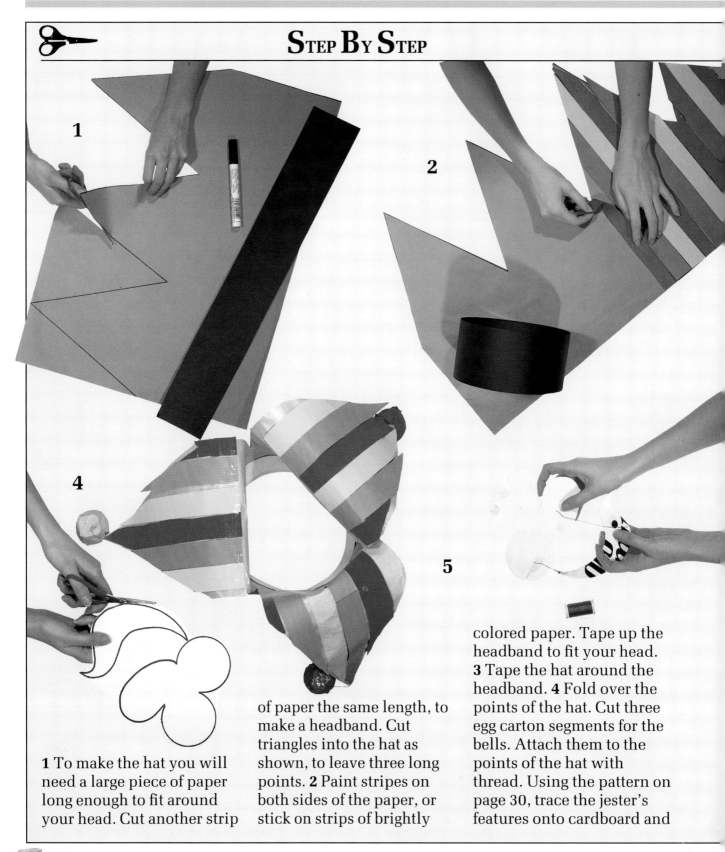

1 To make the hat you will need a large piece of paper long enough to fit around your head. Cut another strip of paper the same length, to make a headband. Cut triangles into the hat as shown, to leave three long points. **2** Paint stripes on both sides of the paper, or stick on strips of brightly colored paper. Tape up the headband to fit your head. **3** Tape the hat around the headband. **4** Fold over the points of the hat. Cut three egg carton segments for the bells. Attach them to the points of the hat with thread. Using the pattern on page 30, trace the jester's features onto cardboard and

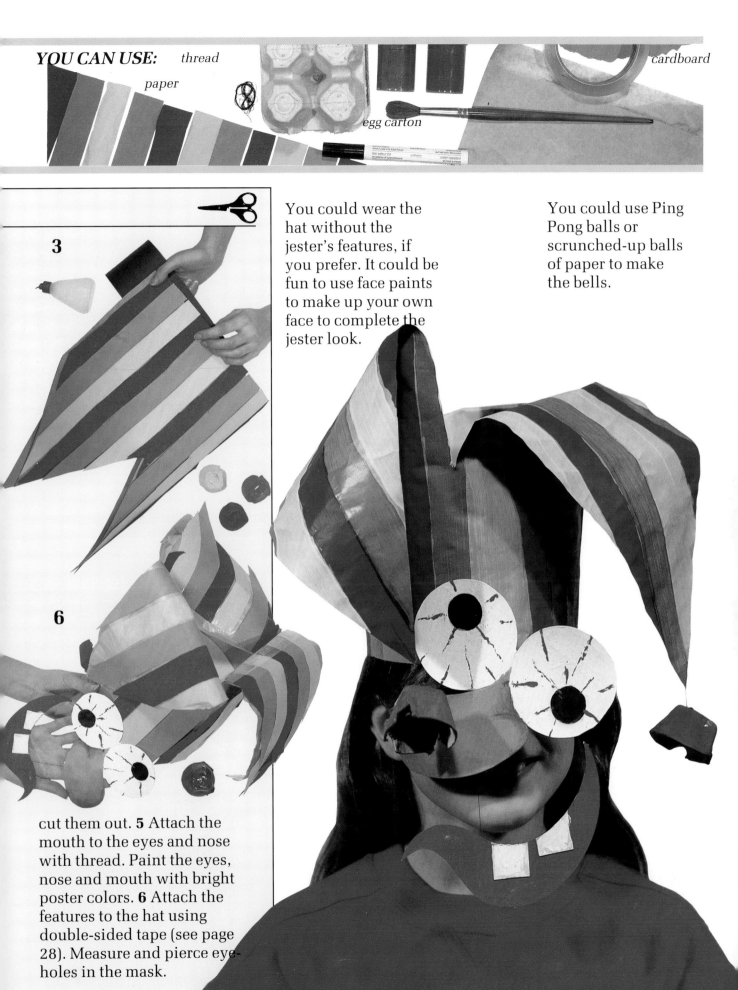

3

6

You could wear the hat without the jester's features, if you prefer. It could be fun to use face paints to make up your own face to complete the jester look.

You could use Ping Pong balls or scrunched-up balls of paper to make the bells.

cut them out. **5** Attach the mouth to the eyes and nose with thread. Paint the eyes, nose and mouth with bright poster colors. **6** Attach the features to the hat using double-sided tape (see page 28). Measure and pierce eye-holes in the mask.

SNAPPING DRAGON

This spectacular mask has a hinged lip which you can raise to reveal a fearsome set of teeth. You can adapt this design to make a dinosaur or a crocodile.

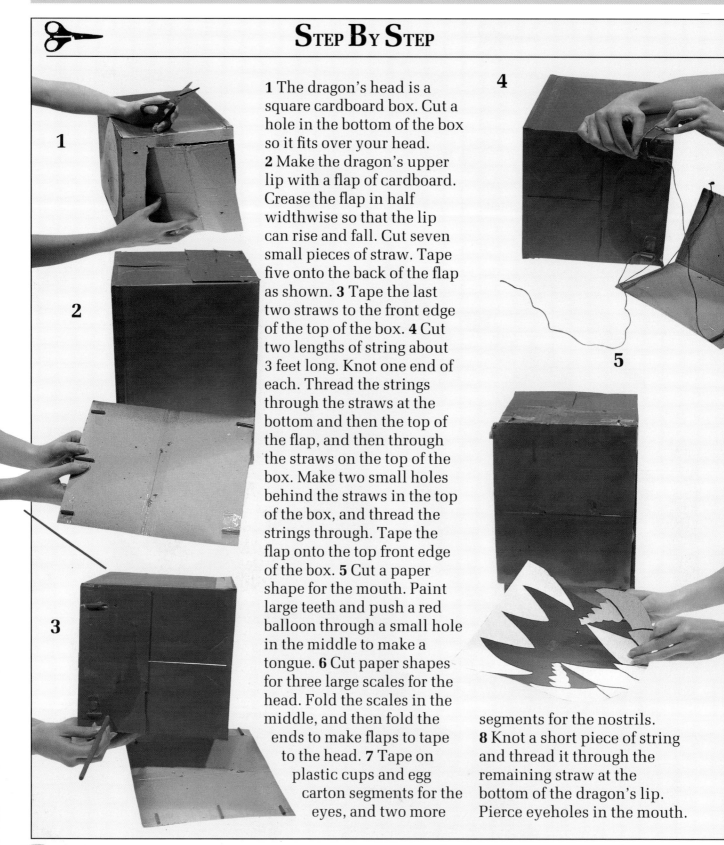

STEP BY STEP

1 The dragon's head is a square cardboard box. Cut a hole in the bottom of the box so it fits over your head. **2** Make the dragon's upper lip with a flap of cardboard. Crease the flap in half widthwise so that the lip can rise and fall. Cut seven small pieces of straw. Tape five onto the back of the flap as shown. **3** Tape the last two straws to the front edge of the top of the box. **4** Cut two lengths of string about 3 feet long. Knot one end of each. Thread the strings through the straws at the bottom and then the top of the flap, and then through the straws on the top of the box. Make two small holes behind the straws in the top of the box, and thread the strings through. Tape the flap onto the top front edge of the box. **5** Cut a paper shape for the mouth. Paint large teeth and push a red balloon through a small hole in the middle to make a tongue. **6** Cut paper shapes for three large scales for the head. Fold the scales in the middle, and then fold the ends to make flaps to tape to the head. **7** Tape on plastic cups and egg carton segments for the eyes, and two more segments for the nostrils. **8** Knot a short piece of string and thread it through the remaining straw at the bottom of the dragon's lip. Pierce eyeholes in the mouth.

YOU CAN USE:

string

cardboard box

balloon

cardboard

egg carton
paper

drinking straws

two plastic cups

6

When you pull on the two strings inside the box, the dragon's upper lip should lift to reveal its teeth; when you pull the short string, the lip will fall again.

7

8

PRACTICAL TIPS

Below are a few practical hints to help you with some of the masks described in this book, and with your craft projects in general.

CREATING FLAPS

Use this whenever you need to fasten tube shapes onto your models. Use scissors to cut a number of short slits into one end of the tube. The slits form a series of flaps around the end. Bend the flaps over, and press the tube flat onto the surface of your model. Attach the flaps to the model with glue, tape or even papier mâché.

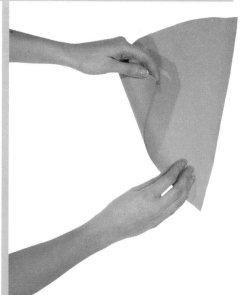

flaps over so that you can tape the cones onto the flat surface of the helmet.

DOUBLE-SIDED TAPE

Double-sided sticky tape is useful when you don't want tape to show on your models. You can buy rolls of this tape in craft and stationery stores, or you can make your own. Cut a short length of tape and roll it over itself until you can stick one end to the other.

MAKING A CONE

To make horns for the Viking helmet on pages 22-23, you need to construct paper cones. You will need pieces of paper about 10 inches square. Roll each piece into a cone, pulling the edge of the paper inside the cone to make a fine point. Tape up the point, and tape along the edge of the rolled paper. Trim the bottom edge of the cone flat with scissors. Cut slits into the bottom edge, to create a series of flaps. Bend the

FABRIC: socks, old clothes or sheets, cloth, felt scraps, and yarn.

MORE JUNK IDEAS

The materials used most often in this book have been paper, cardboard and plastic packaging. Below are some more suggestions about the kinds of junk that can be used to make and decorate your models.

Chestnuts, corks, and eggshells can be used to make eyes, ears, or noses for your masks. Rubber gloves, tin cans, or even socks can form the basis of arms and legs.

NATURAL MATERIALS: twigs, leaves, petals, acorns, nuts, pinecones, bark, shells, pebbles, sponge, cork, feathers.

METAL: soft drink cans, tinfoil, springs, pipe cleaners, coat hangers, paper clips.

RUBBER: rubber bands, balloons, rubber gloves.

PAPER: newspapers, comics and magazines, postcards and birthday cards, unused wallpaper, tissue.

WOOD: spent matches, garden sticks, clothes pegs, cotton spools, popsicle sticks.

PLASTIC: food containers, candy and snack wrappers, buttons, broken toys.

PATTERNS

These patterns will help you with some of the projects in this book.

◄ Use the patterns on page 30 to make the jester's features for pages 24-25.

To use the patterns:
1 Trace the pattern shapes onto tracing paper.
2 Turn the tracing over, and place it on top of paper or cardboard. Scribble over the lines showing through the paper with your pencil. A mirror image of the pattern will appear on the cardboard. **3** If you want the patterns on page 30 to appear the right way round: turn the tracing paper over again, and place it over paper or cardboard.
4 Draw carefully over your image again.

▲ Trace the pattern at the top to make the crow's feathers on pages 18-19.

▶ Use this pattern to make the party masks on pages 18-19. You will find the eyeholes easier to cut out if you push the point of your pencil through the middle of the shape first, to make a hole for your scissors.

INDEX

PRINTED IN BELGIUM BY
proost
INTERNATIONAL BOOK PRODUCTION